10/14

Life Under the Sea
Crabs

by Cari Meister

Bullfrog Books

Ideas for Parents and Teachers

Bullfrog Books let children practice reading informational text at the earliest reading levels. Repetition, familiar words, and photo labels support early readers.

Before Reading

- Ask the child to think about crabs. Ask: What do you know about crabs?
- Look at the picture glossary together. Read and discuss the words.

Read the Book

- Read the book to the child, or have him or her read independently.

After Reading

- Prompt the child to think more. Ask: How are a crab's senses different from yours? What would it be like to walk like a crab?

Bullfrog Books are published by Jump!
5357 Penn Avenue South
Minneapolis, MN 55419
www.jumplibrary.com

Library of Congress Cataloging-in-Publication Data
Meister, Cari.
  Crabs / by Cari Meister.
    p. cm. -- (Bullfrog books. Life under the sea)
  Summary: "This photo-illustrated book for early readers tells the story of a crab looking for food and getting in a fight to defend its territory"-- Provided by publisher.
  Audience: K to grade 3.
  Includes bibliographical references and index.
  ISBN 978-1-62031-032-8 (hardcover : alk. paper) --
ISBN 978-1-62496-050-5 (ebook)
  1. Crabs--Juvenile literature. 2. Crabs--Behavior-- Juvenile literature. I. Title.
  QL444.M33M44 2014
  595.3'86--dc23   2013001958

Series Editor   Rebecca Glaser
Book Designer   Ellen Huber
Photo Researcher   Heather Dreisbach

Photo Credits: Dreamstime, 7, 17, 24; Fotolia, 10, 14–15; Getty, 4, 9, 16, 23tr; iStockphoto, 5, 6; Shutterstock, cover, 3, 8, 12, 13, 19, 20–21, 22, 23bl, 23br; SuperStock, 13, 23tl; Veer, 11

Printed in the United States of America at Corporate Graphics, North Mankato, Minnesota.
5-2013 / PO 1003

10 9 8 7 6 5 4 3 2 1

Table of Contents

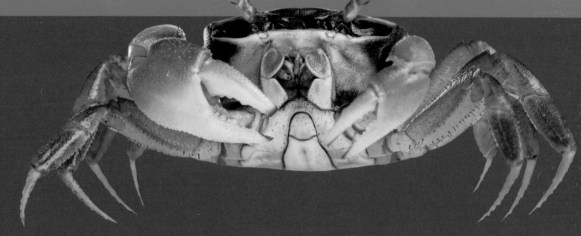

Hiding in the Sand

Who is hiding
in the sand?

A crab!

Do you see its antennas?

antenna

They help smell.

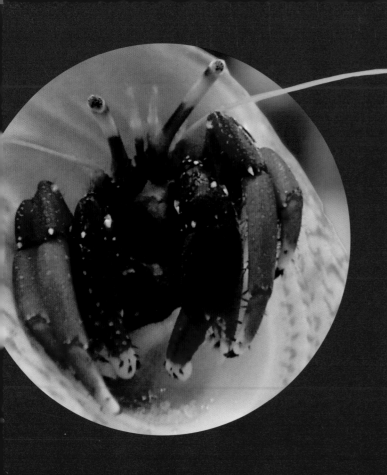

Is there danger?
No. It's safe.
A little crab climbs out.

He walks sideways.

eyestalk ·······▶

A crab's eyes
are on eyestalks.

They turn.

This helps it
see well.

11

A snail! Yum!

Crabs also eat mussels and fish. Sometimes they eat other crabs!

Oh no! What's this?
A big crab waves his claw.

Go away little crab!
This is my spot!

The crabs fight.
The big crab
grabs the little
crab's claw.

It comes off!
Is he okay?

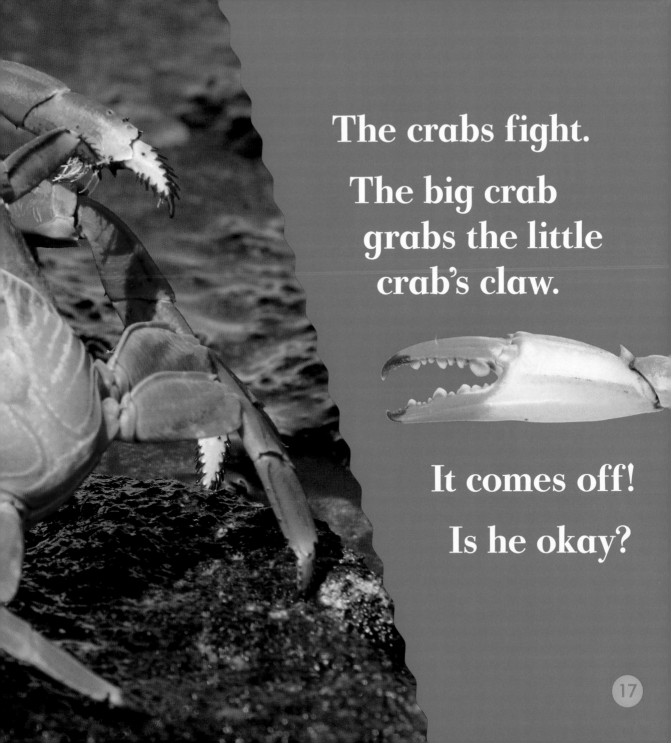

17

The little
crab hides.

He will live.

In time,
a new claw
will grow.

The big crab wins!

Parts of a Crab

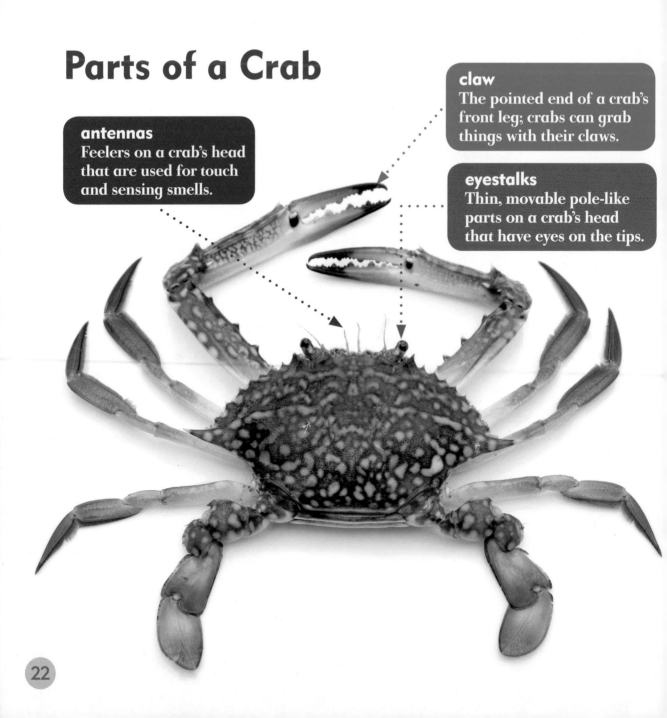

claw
The pointed end of a crab's front leg; crabs can grab things with their claws.

antennas
Feelers on a crab's head that are used for touch and sensing smells.

eyestalks
Thin, movable pole-like parts on a crab's head that have eyes on the tips.

Picture Glossary

danger
When it is not safe; animals are in danger when another animal might eat them.

sideways
Moving to the side.

mussels
A kind of shellfish you can eat.

snail
A soft animal with a slimy body that has a shell on its back.

Index

To Learn More

Learning more is as easy as 1, 2, 3.

1) Go to www.factsurfer.com

2) Enter "crab" into the search box.

3) Click the "Surf" button to see a list of websites.

With factsurfer.com, finding more information is just a click away.